Creative Coloring

Insect Designs
Coloring Book

Copyright © 2017 by Creative Coloring Press
All rights reserved. This book or any portion thereof
may not be reproduced or used in any manner whatsoever without the express written permission of the publisher
except for the use of brief quotations in a book review.

First edition: 2017

Disclaimer/Limit of Liability
This book is for informational purposes only. The views expressed are those of the author alone, and should not be taken
as expert, legal, or medical advice. The reader is responsible for his or her own actions.

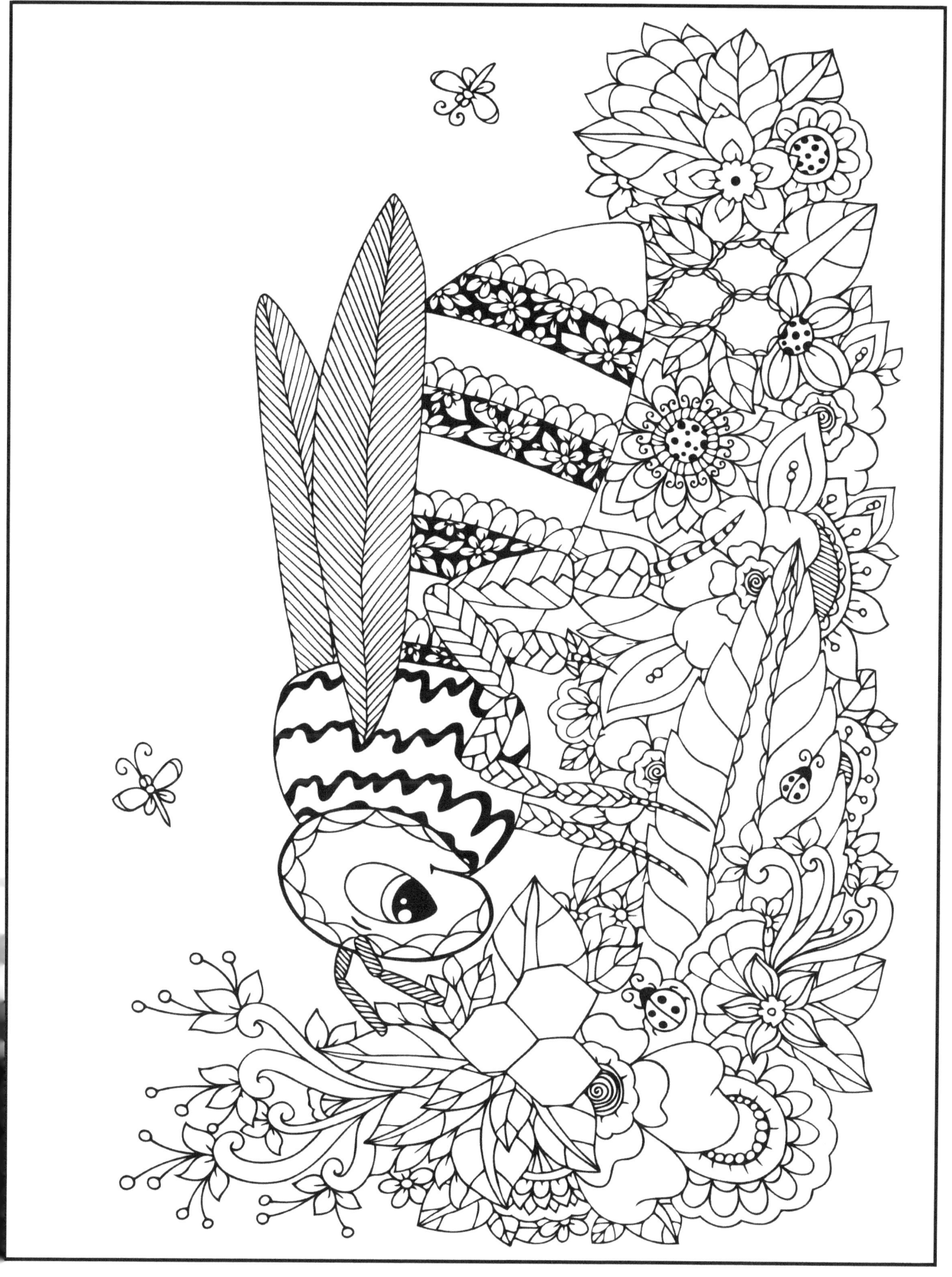

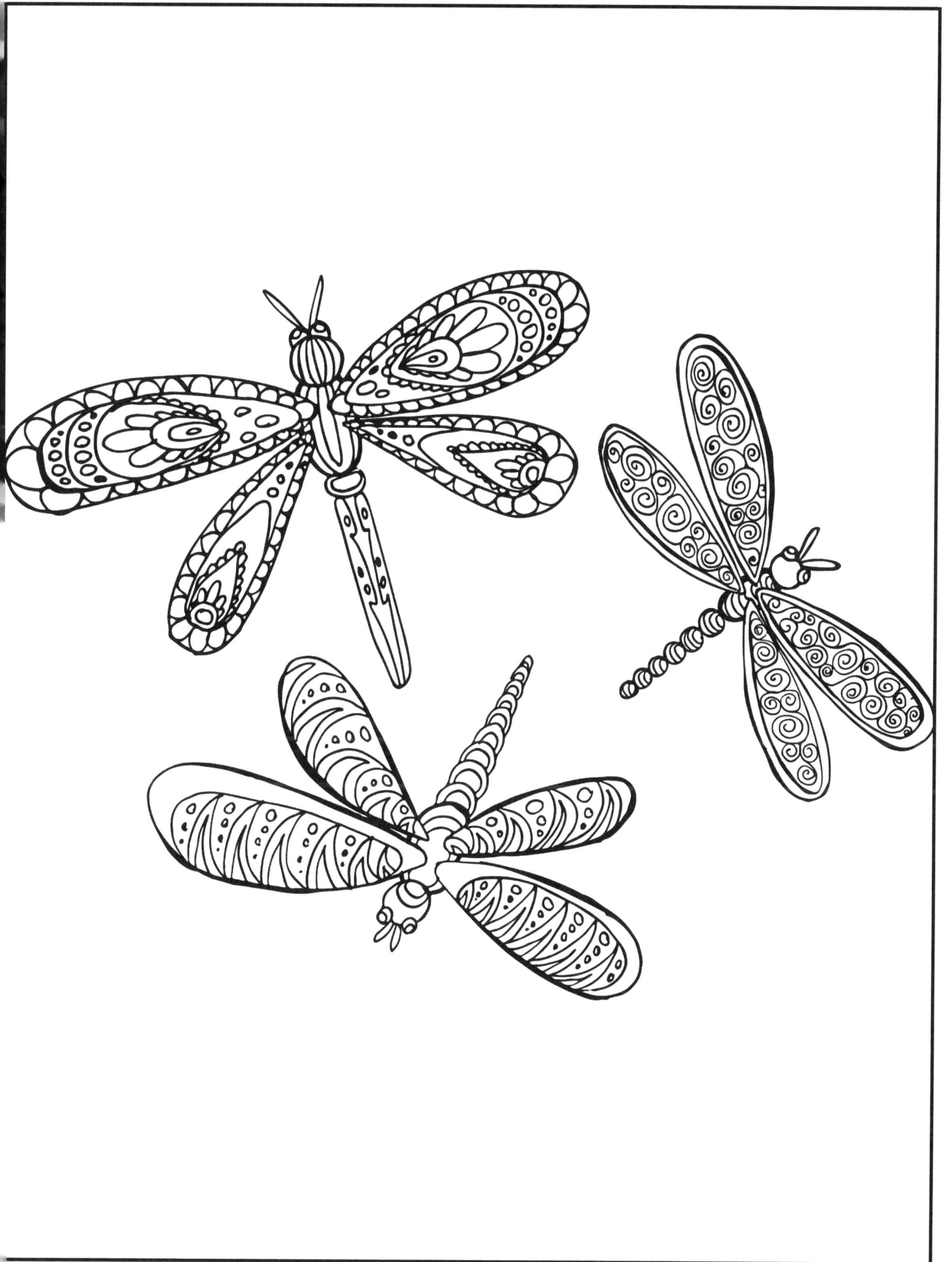

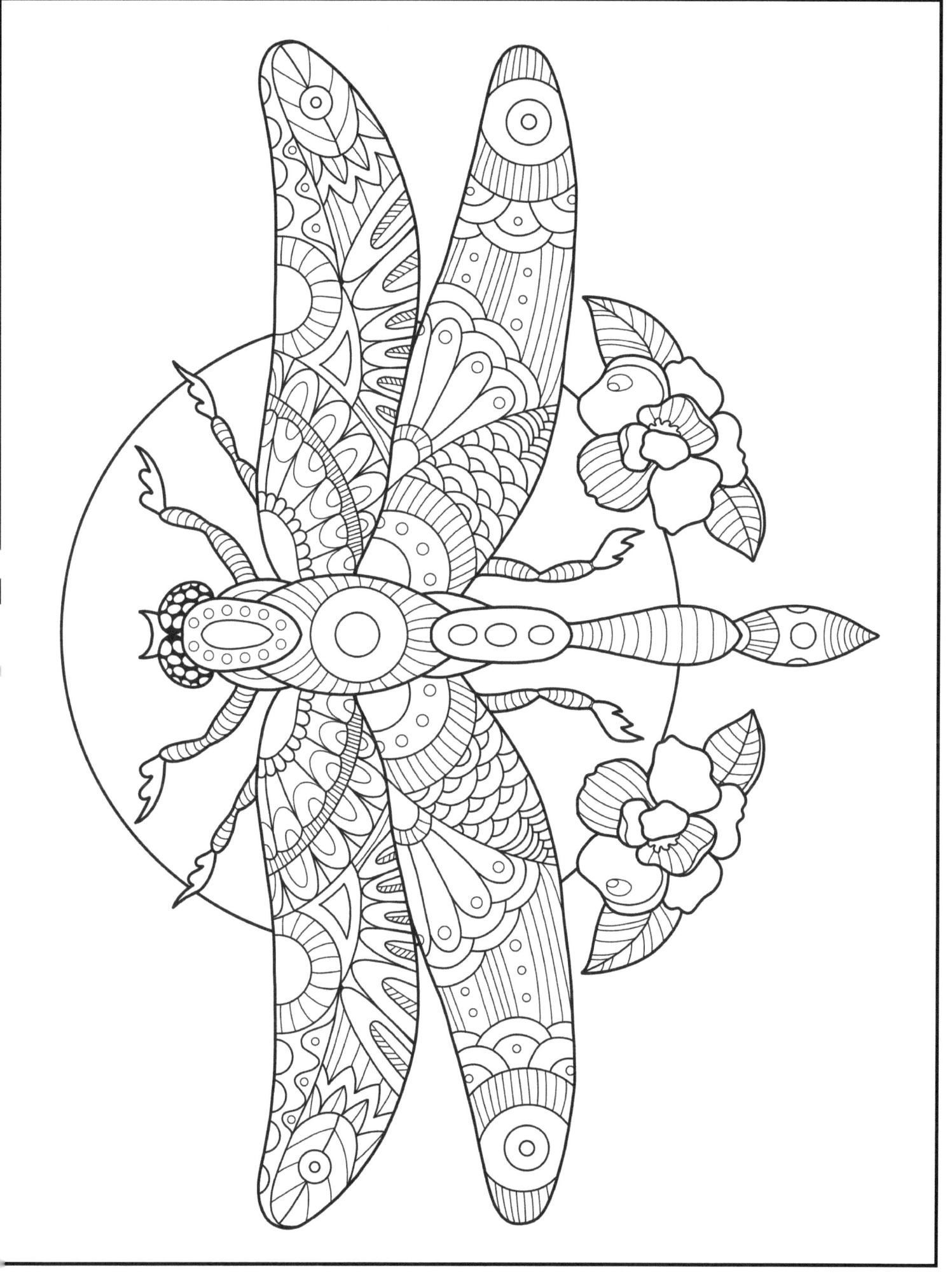

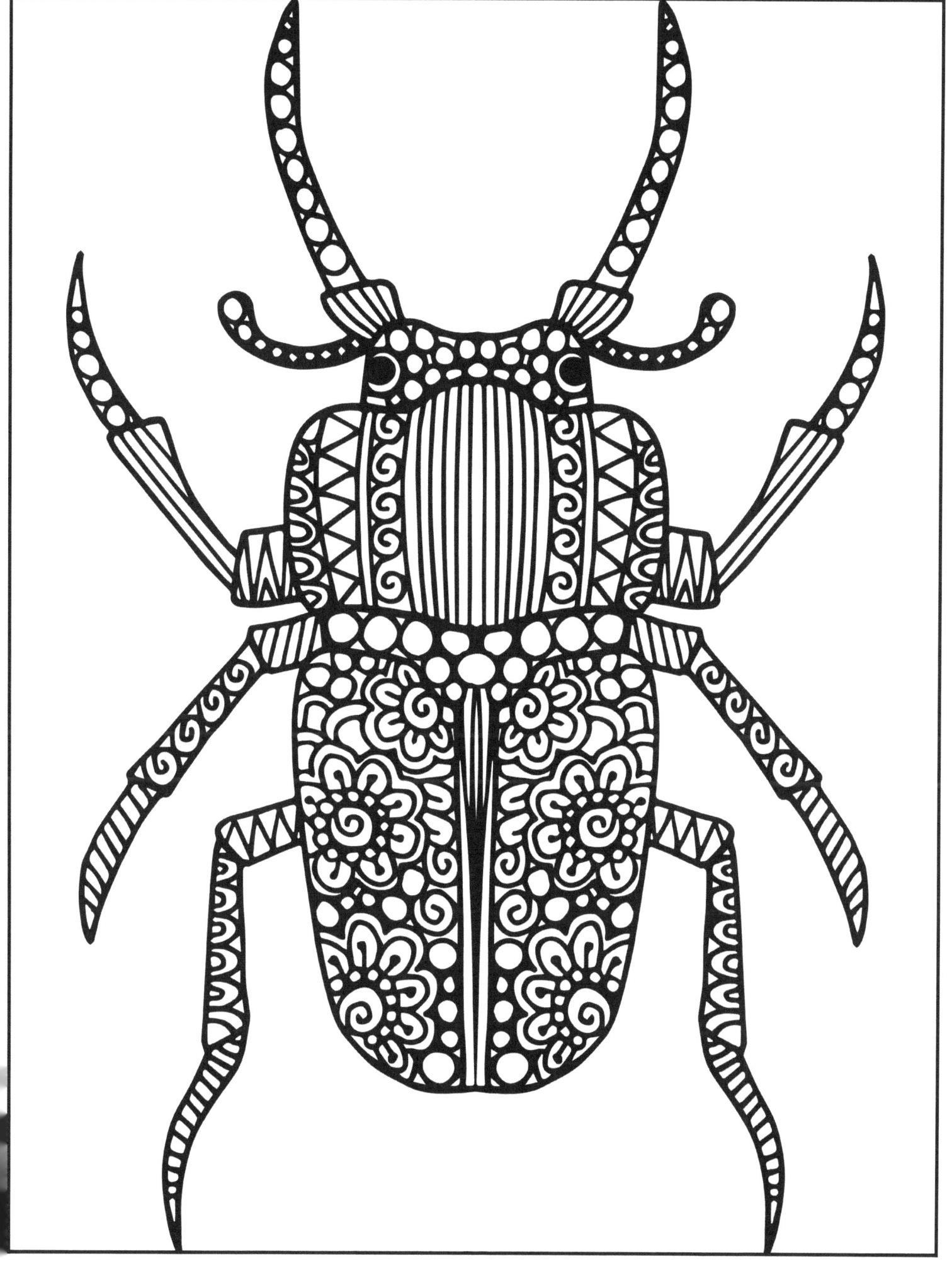

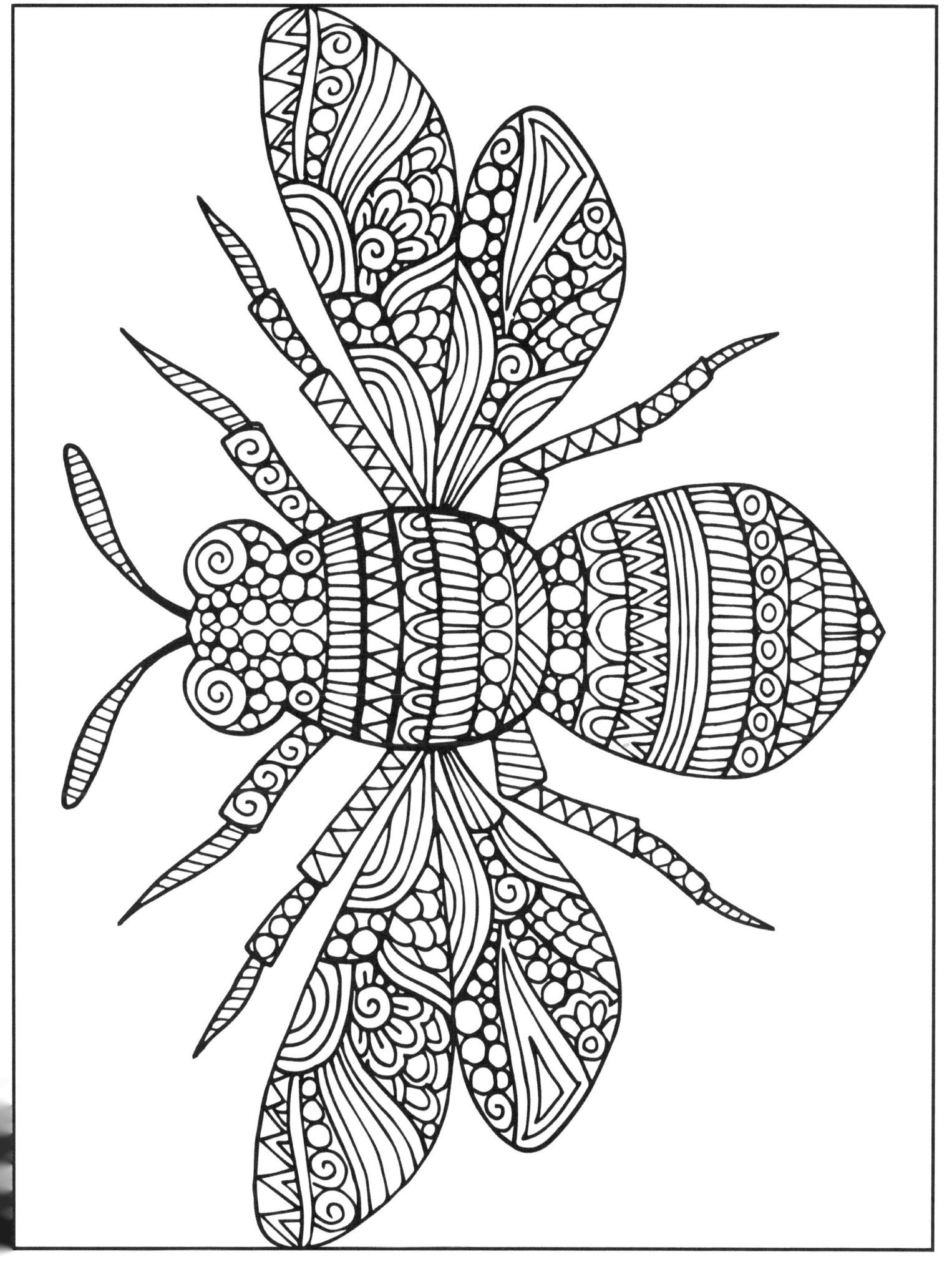

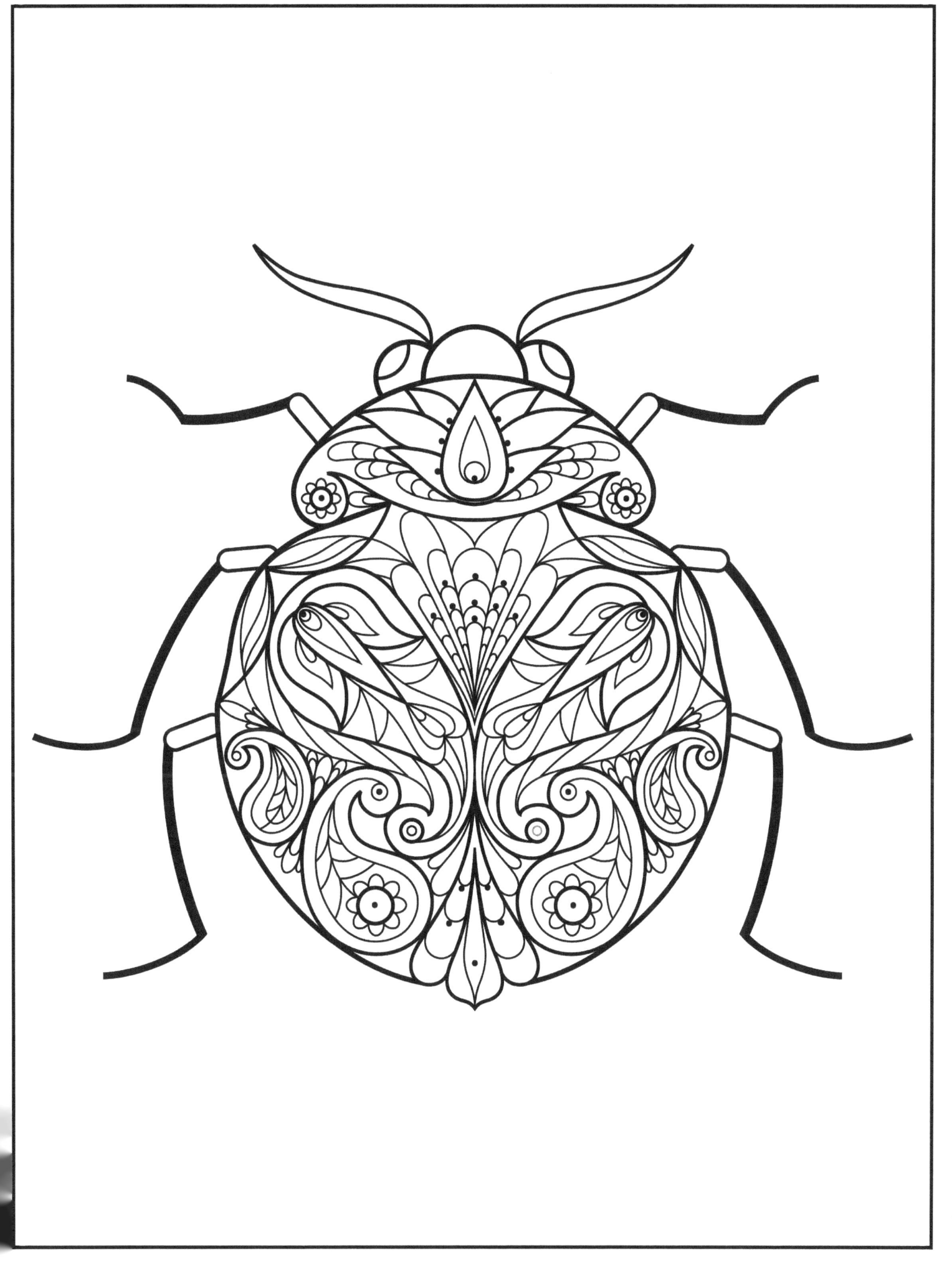

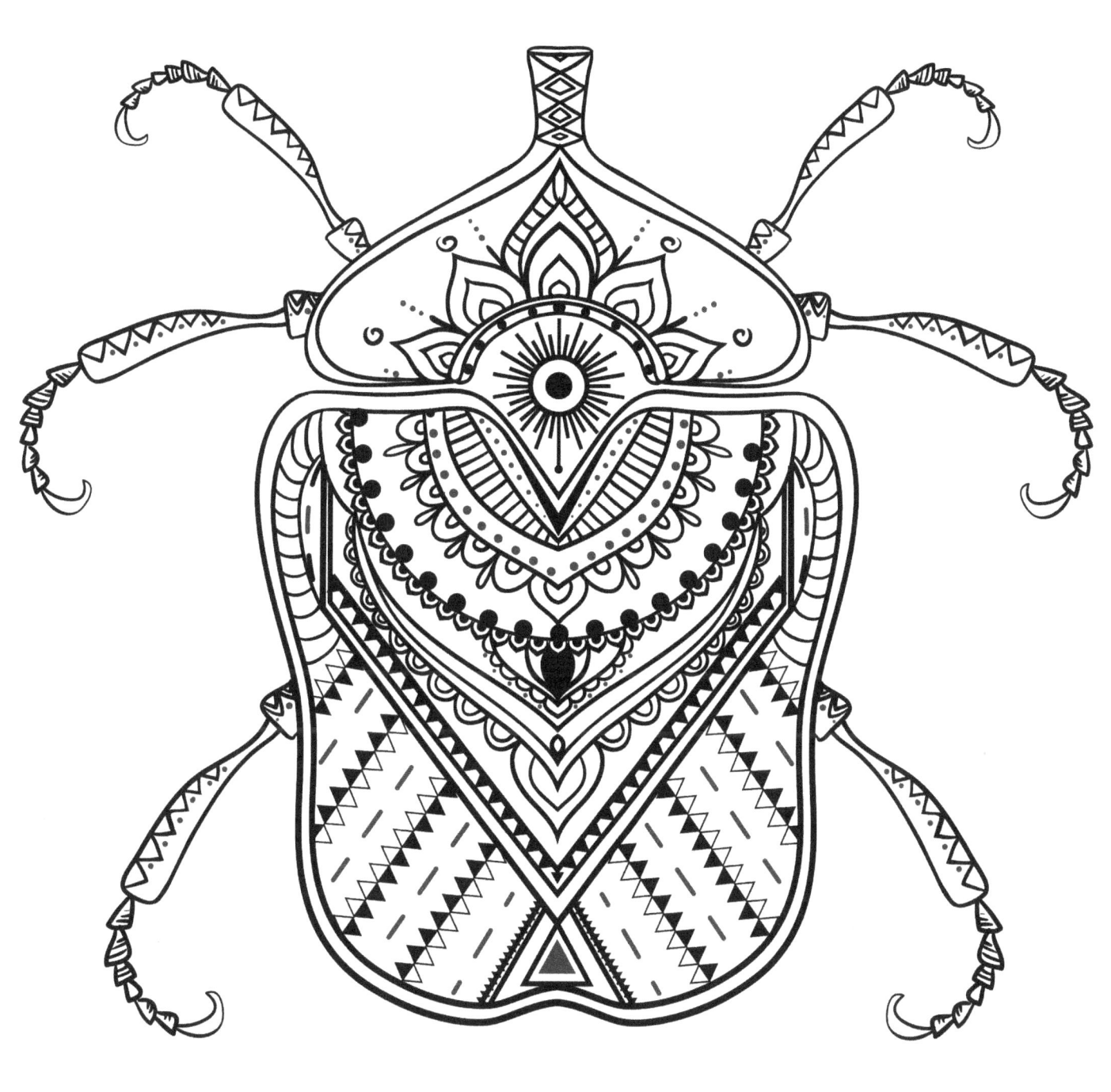

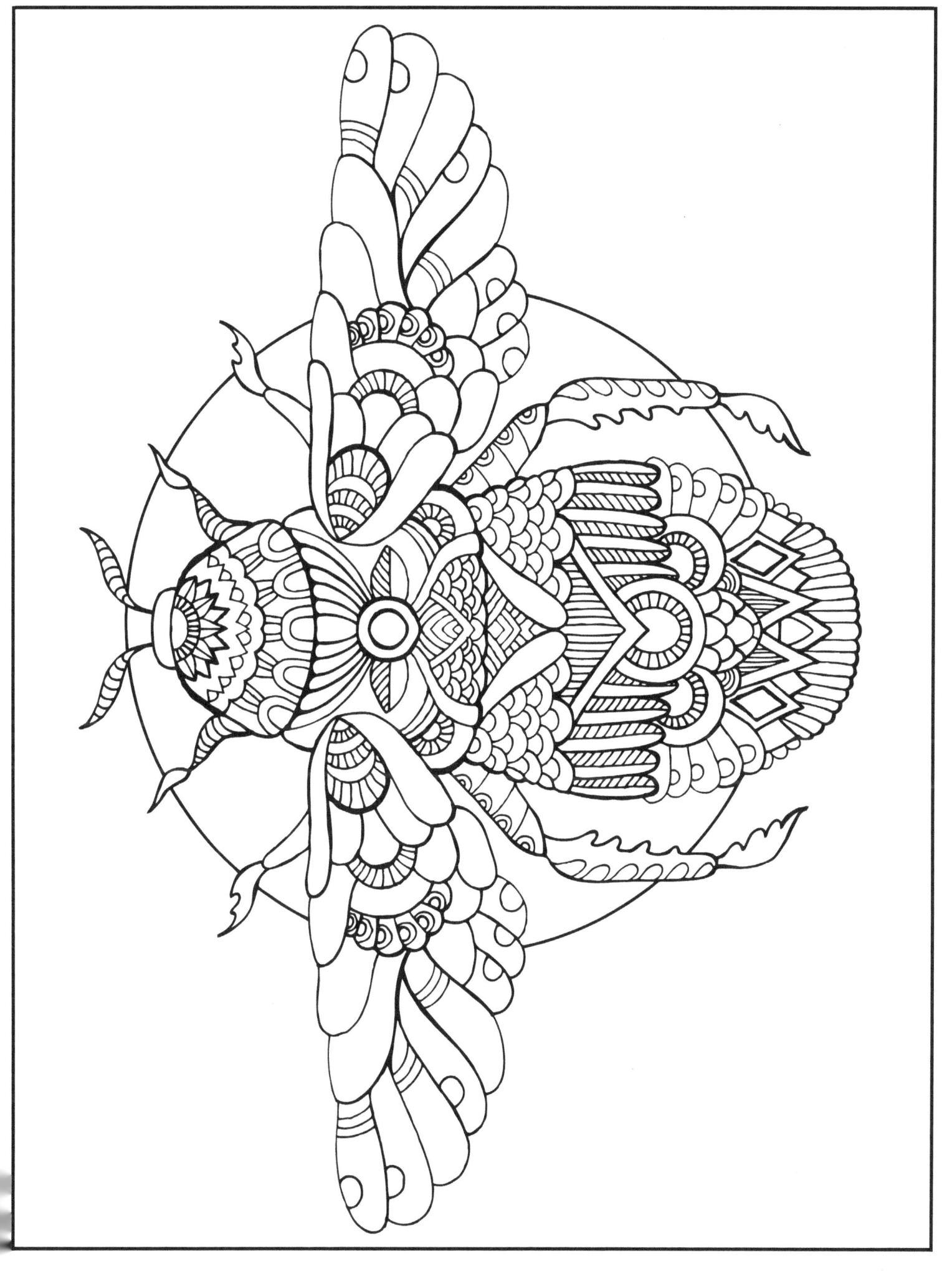

Thank you for purchasing this coloring book! I hope that you enjoy coloring it as much as I enjoyed creating it. Please consider leaving a review, I really appreciate hearing your opinion!

Sign-Up to Get a Free Coloring Book

Subscribe to our newsletter and get a free printable coloring book of some of our most popular illustrations. Plus you'll receive special offers, sneak peeks at new releases, and more. Visit us at **www.creativecoloring.co** for details.

We want to hear from you!

We hope you've enjoyed this coloring book and that is brings you many hours of fun, stress relief, and creativity. We'd love to see and share your creations.

Send us your ideas, suggestions, and finished artwork:

www.creativecoloring.co
facebook.com/creativecoloringpress
Instagram: @creativecoloringpress
Twitter: @creativecoloringpress

Bonus

Turn the page for bonus pages from some of our most popular coloring books.

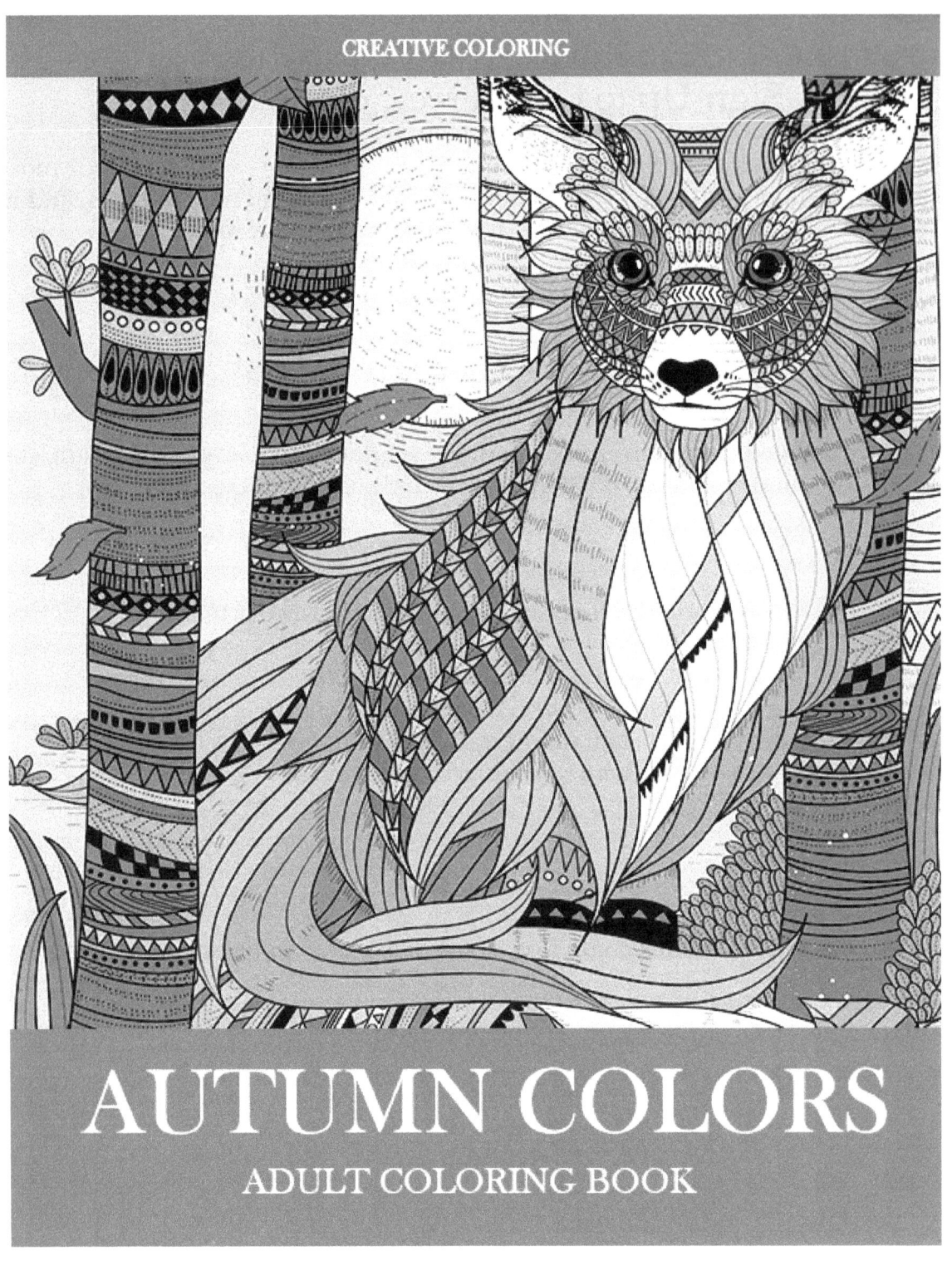

Aautumn Colors Adult Coloring Book by Creative Coloring Press.
Available now at Amazon.com, Barnes and Noble, and other online retailers.

Aautumn Colors Adult Coloring Book by Creative Coloring Press.
Available now at Amazon.com, Barnes and Noble, and other online retailers.

CREATIVE COLORING PRESS

DRAGON
COLORING BOOK FOR ADULTS

INCLUDES 38 DAZZLING DRAGON DESIGNS TO COLOR

Aautumn Colors Adult Coloring Book by Creative Coloring Press. Available now at Amazon.com, Barnes and Noble, and other online retailers.

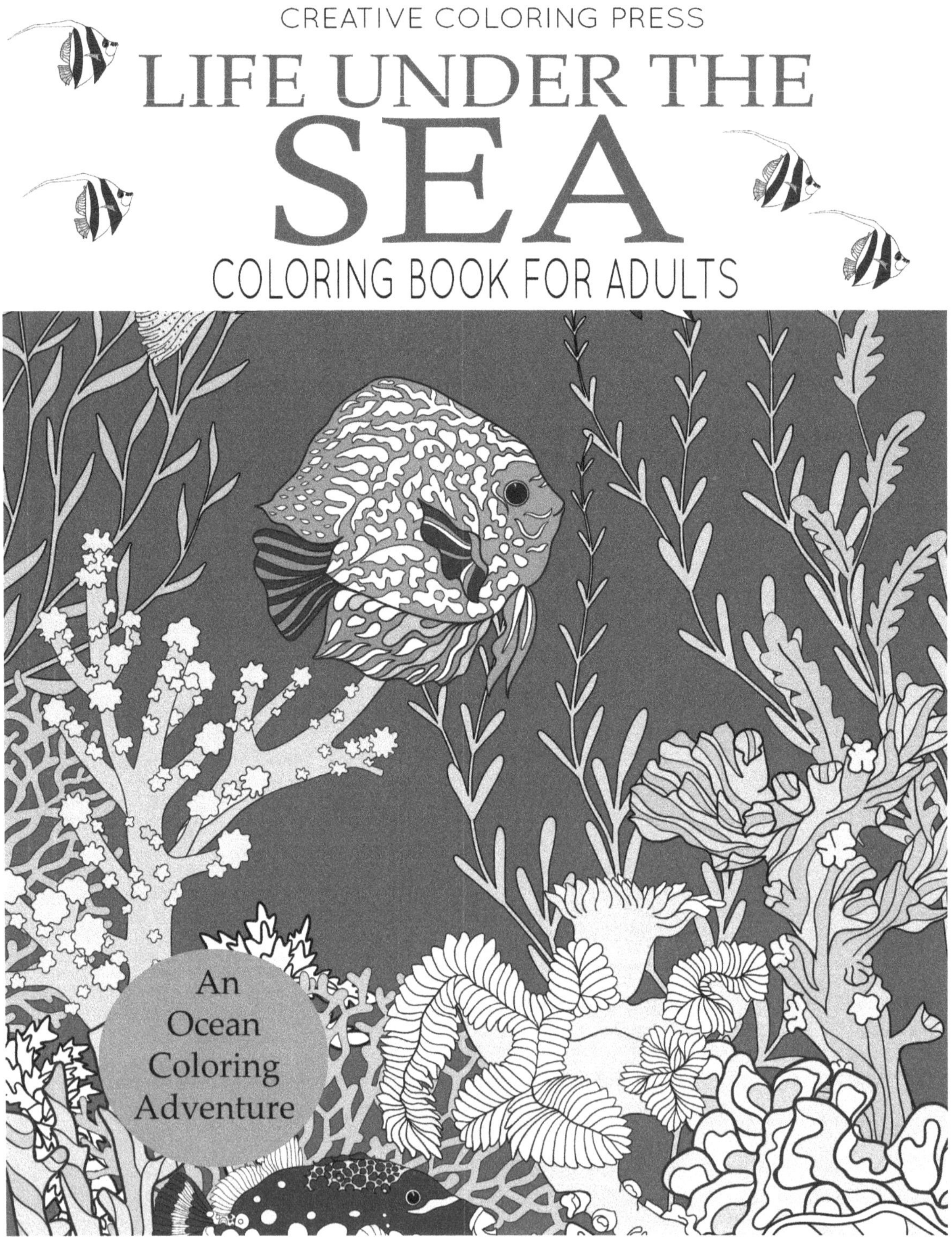

CREATIVE COLORING PRESS
LIFE UNDER THE SEA
COLORING BOOK FOR ADULTS

An Ocean Coloring Adventure

Aautumn Colors Adult Coloring Book by Creative Coloring Press.
Available now at Amazon.com, Barnes and Noble, and other online retailers.

www.ingramcontent.com/pod-product-compliance
Lightning Source LLC
Chambersburg PA
CBHW081202020426
42333CB00020B/2604